FRAGMENTS OF 'CHRONICLE'

Hippolytus of Thebes

Translated by: D.P. Curtin
Edited by: Celina Rhodes

Dalcassian
Publishing
Company

PHILADELPHIA, PA

ISBN: 978-1-960069-60-3 (Paperback)
ISBN: 978-1-960069-61-0 (Hardback)

Library of Congress Control Number:
Author: Curtin, D.P. (1985-)

Front cover image: *Basilica of St. Vitalis, Ravenna, Republic of Italy*
Book design by J.J. Ripplestick

Printed by Ingram Content Group, 1 Ingram Blvd, La Vergne, Tennessee

First printing edition 2023.

Conſtantinopel

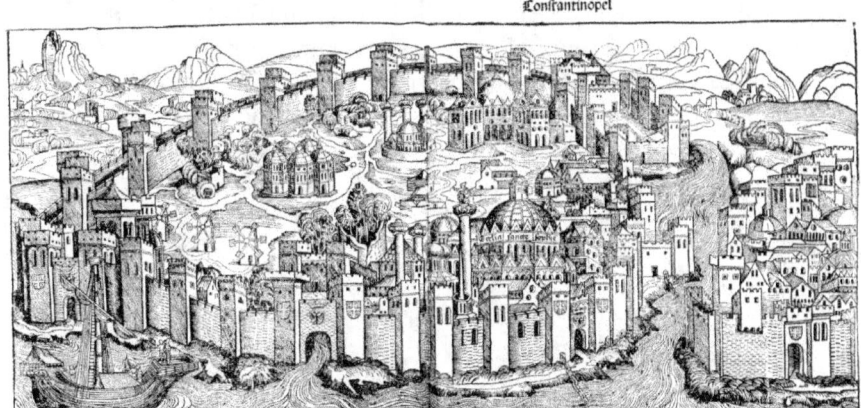

Introduction

Commonly, it surprises the general public that we have an incomplete perspective on the past; that the task of historical chronology is one that is evolving over time, and the dates that are assigned to historical events in antiquity are not necessarily permanently affixed. The task of reconstructing the past to fit in a coherent, linear model is something that is particularly Hellenic, and there is no shortage of examples of this in surviving Greek texts. However, our view of the past is always limited by those artifacts and texts that survive. There is no pure sense of an uncomplicated history, one that isn't obscured by changes in the chronographer, or collapses in whole civilizations. Our window into the past is fractured and heavily dependent on the skill and interest of some ancient copyist.

Many texts survive, but there is a larger catalog which have been lost or are only found in the citations of later writers. The works of Hippolytus of Thebes fit into this category, as the only elements of his works that have come down to us from antiquity are found in the text of other Byzantine writers. The length of his magnum opus and the exact nature of its subject is unknown. In its surviving fragments, Hippolytus appears to be interested in the family of Christ, the reign of the Emperor Constantine, and the accumulation of years between various biblical events. The source of his material is also a curiosity, and where it is cited, appears to at least partially differ from that of Ephipanius of Salamis concerning the family of Christ. Nonetheless, his construction of family life in 1st century Judea is entirely credible. It is possible that he was drawing upon some unknown source of a tradition about the family of Christ which has now been lost. However, there should be some caution assumed with this reasoning, as it is entirely made ex nihilo.

Little is known about his life, although he is frequently confused with his more famous Latin namesake, Hippolytus of Rome. He appears to have written in Greek during the Heraclian dynasty, when the vernacular language of the empire continued to shift away from Latin. Fr. Jacques Paul Migne, the French Catholic priest, collected these works for his own work, the Patrologia Graeca, in the late 19th century. The Latin in the preceding translation is taken directly from the Migne collection, which is also a translation from the 8th century Greek. While this work has been translated into German by Franz Diekamp in 1898, there is no prior translation into the English tongue, and despite its utility, it remains a largely obscure text to the academic world. To date, no critical scholarship has delved into these fragments in any serious manner, although they are frequently cited by scholars looking to establish a chronology for the events of the New Testament.

D.P. Curtin
June 15, 2023
Johnstown, PA

FRAGMENT I

Hippolytus of Thebans in his commentary on the Chronicle of the genealogy of our Lord Jesus Christ:
Therefore, our Lord Jesus Christ was incarnated in the year 5500[1].

He was born under the Emperor Augustus in a cave on the 25th of December.

From Adam to Noah in the year 2242.
From Noah to Abraham in 1170 years.
From Abraham until Moses in 404 years.
From Moses to David in 599 years.
From David to Christ in 1045 years, at the same time 5500 years [from creation].

From the incarnation of Christ until the coming of the Magi, two years.
From the flight into Egypt until the death of Herod, the son of Antipater, three years.

They lived in Egypt at Heliopolis near Memphis for three years.
But after their return to Galilee, until the death of Archelaus was nineteen years.

When Archelaus died in the 88th year[2], and Augustus in the 56th year of his reign[3].

From the death of Archelaus until the baptism of Christ, three years, and at the same time 30 years [of his life].

---

[1] This appears to be dating from the largely forgotten Anno Mundi calendar that is dating time from the alleged creation of the world.
[2] Herod Archaeleus died in the year 6 AD, when the Judean tetrarchy collapsed. It is unclear what this would be the 88th year of, as it would have been around the year 82 BC
[3] They must be asserting that he held civic power since the death of his uncle, Julius Caesar, in the year 44 BC.

From the baptism of Christ until the stoning of Zachariah, it was a single year.

But from the death of Zachariah until the death of his own son, John, under Herod the younger[4], the son of Archelaus, who was in prison one year.
From the death of John until the saving passion, six months.
For John the Baptist lived thirty-three years, thirty indeed in the wilderness, but in three years, he baptized in the Jordan, preaching penance. Thus, our Lord Jesus Christ lived thirty years in His youth. But after His baptism, He chose His disciples to proclaim His kingdom, until the cross was three years.

Whence, the Fathers in the Council of Nicaea decreed that priests should not be ordained before thirty years of age and that it is sufficient for a disciple to be like a teacher. For the servant is to be like his master. From the saving passion and ascension, until the stoning of Stephen was seven years, and from that time until the light that appeared to Paul was six months.

From Paul's baptism and preaching until the most immaculate assumption of our Lord, there are three years together, and about forty-four years in total.

For the Deipara[5], the purest among men, lived in the temple for fourteen years and in the house of Joseph for four months. When the announcement was made to her, she conceived and gave birth to our Lord Jesus Christ, together for fifteen years.

From the incarnation of Christ, He lived thirty-three years. Until the assumption of Christ in the house of John in the year eleven, for she lived beyond thirty-three years. Whence, our lesson is to be retained. So, all His years are fifty-nine.

---

[4] Herod Antipas, who reigned 4 BC to 39 AD, who was brother, not the son of Herod Archaeleus.
[5] That is to say, the Virgin Mary

Moreover, John, whom Christ loved, and was a virgin and an evangelist, remained in Jerusalem in his house; the mother of the churches, to which the apostles fled because of the fear of the Jews.

There, the Passover was also prepared and the first mystery was delivered to the disciples; the Lord appeared to them there after the resurrection; the Holy Spirit fell upon the disciples there; Thomas showed the types of nails; the apostles ordained as the first bishop, the son of Joseph, the brother of the Lord, not the son of Zebedee, the brother of John. For Zebedee was called having his own ship, and the chief, who were in there were Galileans. He was the first of the men.

But after the death of Zebedee, John left his father's lands in Galilee and procured a home in Jerusalem. Whence, it is said of him that he was known to the high priest. There, he received the most holy Deipara into his house until her assumption, and afterwards, when he had preached the word, he was taken up.

James, having become the first bishop of Jerusalem, is indeed said to be the brother of the Lord according to the flesh, but the son of Joseph the carpenter by his carnal wife. For he had four sons; Joseph, James, Simon, Judah, and two daughters, Esther and Martha by his wife Salome. Salome was the daughter of Haggai, brother of Zachariah, who, in turn, was the father of John [the Baptist], and the son of Berechiah, the son of Abijah the priest.

And then indeed, Joseph was a widower; so much so that John the Baptist and Salome were the children of true brothers. Haggai, son of Berechiah, was John's uncle. Similarly, Zachariah, the brother of Haggai, was the uncle of Salome, the wife of Joseph the carpenter. There were, moreover, in our holy Lord Deipara from Bethlehem. Three sisters from Bethlehem; the daughter of Mathan the priest and Marice[6], his wife, during the reign of Cleopatra and

---

[6] An alternate spelling for the name Mary

Sapora the Persian[7], before the reign of Herod Antipater. The first was Mary; the second, Sobe; the third, Anne. So, she married first in Bethlehem and gave birth to Salome, a midwife. And the second likewise went to Bethlehem and gave birth to Elizabeth; and the third in the land of Galilee and begat Mary, the Mother of God.

Wherefore, Salome the midwife, Elisabeth, and Saint Deipara are the daughters of three sisters, and John the Baptist and our Lord were cousins. Christ indeed.

He is said to be the son of Joseph, both because he nursed him together with his sons, and also because he was related to Haggai, the brother of Zechariah the priest, the son of Barachirm.

Hippolyti Thebani en commentario ejus Chronico de prosapia Domini nostri Jesu Chrsiti:
Incarnatus igitur est Dominus noster Jesu Christus anno 5500.

Sub Augusto imperatore natus est in spelunca, mense Decembris die 25.
Ab Adam usque ad Noe anni 2242.
Et a Noe usque ad Abraham anni 1170.
Et ab Abraham usque ad Moyses anni 444,
Et a Moyses usque ad David anni 599
Et a David usque ad Christum anni 1045, simul anni 5500.
À Christi incarnatione autem usque ad Magorum adventum anni duo.
Et a fuga in Egyptum usque ad mortem Herodis filii Antipatri anni tres.
Habitarunt in Egypto Heliopoli juxta Memphia annis 3.
A regressu vero ipsorum ad propria in Gali- leam, usque ad mortem Archelai anni 19.
Cum Archelao moritur et Augustus anno 88, regni 56.
A morte vero Archelai usque ad baptismum Christian. 3, simul an 30.

---

[7] There is no Persian king by this name. They might be referring to Pacorus I, King of Parthia.

A baptismate autem Christi usque ad lapidatio- nem Zacharis anunus

A morte vero Zacharie usque ad Joannis filii ipsius mortem, sub Herode juniore Archelai filio in carcere patratam an. unus.

Et a morte Joannis usque ad salvificam passionem menses 6.

Vixit enim Joannes Baptista annis 33, triginta quidem in eremo; tribus vero annis baptizavit in Jordane praedicans penitentiam. Sicque Dominus noster Jesus Christus triginta annis in juventute vixit.

Post baptismum vero elegit discipulos, ut pro- dicarent regnum suum, usque crucem annis 3.

Unde Patres in Nicena synodo statuerunt, ut non ordinarentur presbyteri ante triginta annos, dixeruntque sufficere discipulo, ut sit sicut magister; et servo, ut sit sicut dominus ejus.

A salvifica vero passione, et ascensione, usque ad Stephani lapidationem anni 7, et ab illa usque ad lucem, que Paulo apparuit, menses sex.

Et a Pauli baptismate ac praedicatione usque ad Domine nostre perquam immaculate assumptionem sunt anni tres simul anni 44.

Vixit enim inter homines purissima Deipara in templo annis 14, in domo Joseph mensibus 4, et annuntiatio ei facta est, concepit, peperitque Dominum nostrum Jesum Christum, simul annis 15.

Ab incarnatione vero Christi vixit annos 33.

Usque ad assumptionem Christi in domo Joannis anni 11.

Ita ut omnes ejus anni sint 59.

Porro hic est Joannes, quem diligebat Christus, fuitque virgo et evangelista, mansit Hierosolymis in domo sua, Ecclesiarum matre, ad quam confugerunt apostoli, propter metum Judzeorum.

Ibi praeparatum fuit et Pascha : ibi primo mysterium discipulis traditum fuit: ibi post resurrectionem Dominus illis apparuit ; ibi Spiritus sanctus illapsus est discipulis: ibi Thomse ostendit typos clavorum: ibi apostoli in primum episcopum ordinarunt filium Josephi, fratrem Domini, non folium Zebedzei, fratrem Joannis, Zebedeus enim propriam navem habens appellatur, et precipuo- rum, qui in Galileea erant, virorum fuit primus.

Post mortem vero (Zebedzi) Joannes patris sui horeditatem distraxit in Galila, et Hierosolymis domicilium comparavit, unde ut dicitur de ipso, erat notus pontifici.

Hic recepit sanctissimam Deiparam in domum suam usque ad resurrectionem ipsius, et postea cum praedicasset verbum, et ipse assumptus est.

Jacobus autem factus primus episcopus Jeroso- lymitanus, frater quidem Domini secundum carnem esse dicitur, filius vero fabri Josephi ex carnali uxore ejus. Quatuor enim filios habuit Joseph, Jacobum, Simonem, Judam et Joseph: et duas filias Esther et Martham ex uxore sua Salome, quae fuit filia Aggsi fratris Zacharim, patris Joannis, filii Barachie, filii Abis sacerdotis.

Et tunc. quidem viduus erat Joseph: adeo ut Joannes Baptista et Salome sint fratrum germano- rum liberi. Aggseus cnim Barachie filius, erat patruus Joannis. Similiter et Zacharias frater Aggei patruus Salomes uxoris Josephi fabri. Erant porro sancte Domine nostre Deiparae ex Bethleem tres sorores a Bethleem filie Mathan sacerdotis, et Marice uxoris ejus regnante Cleopatra et Sapore Persa, ante regnum Herodis Antipatri. Prima nomen erat Maria ; secunda vero Sobe; terti: autem Ann. Nupsit igitur prima in Bethleem, et genuit Salomen obstetricem. Secunda autem similiter in Bethleem, et genuit Elisabeth; et tertia in terra Galilz:e, et genuit Mariam Matrem Dei. Quare Salome obstetrix, Elissbeth, et sancta Deipara suntrium sororum filie: atque hinc Joannes Baptista et Dominus noster erant consobrini. Christus vero filius Josephi dicitur, tum quod una cum filiis suis eum nutriebat, et tum quod erat ex cognatione Aggei fratris Zacharie sacerdotis, filii Barachirm.

FRAGMENT II

And we find in the divine Scriptures that in the sixteenth year of her life, the most blessed Lady Deipara gave birth to our Savior and Lord Jesus Christ. Indeed, she was baptized by the apostles Peter and John, whom Christ had baptized. Indeed, after the salvific suffering of Deipara, she lived eleven years, and all the duration of her life was sixty-one years. And the divine John the Theologian also lived until the reign of Domitian, Emperor of the Romans[8], so much so that the whole period of his life was one hundred and ten years[9].

Invenimus autem in divina Scriptura, quod decimo sexto anno statis sue sauctissima Domina Deipara Salvatorem et Dominum nostrum Jesum Christum pepererit; baptizata vero sit a Petro, et Joanne apostolis, ipsos autem baptizarit Christus. Vixit vero post salvificam passionem Deipara annos xi, fueruntque omnes totius vitæ ejus anni sexaginta unus. Vixit autem et divus Joannes Theologus usque ad Domitianum imperatorem Romanorum, adeo ut omne vite ejus tempus sit centum et decem annorum.

[8] That is to say between 81 and 96 AD.
[9] Assuming that John was killed then during the last year of the reign of Domitian, the earliest his birth would have been, according to Hippolytus was 14 BC.

FRAGMENT III

The most holy patriarch of Jerusalem, the great Sophronius[10], celebrating John the Evangelist, taught in the Church of God[11], that the father of [John] the Theologian was Zebedee, and his mother was Salome, the daughter of Joseph. [He, Joseph] had four sons, and three daughters. The sons were James, Simon, Judah, and Joseph, and the daughters were Esther[12], Martha[13], and Salome, who was the wife of Zebedee, the mother of John. Therefore, the Savior was John's uncle, as the brother of Joseph's daughter, Salome.

Sanctissimus autem patriarcha Hierosolymorum magnus Sophronius encomio celebrans Joannem evangelistam docet Ecclesiam Dei, quod pater The- ologi exstitit Zebedeus, mater vero illius Salome, ipsa fllia Josephi, qui Josephus quatuor habuit filios, filias tres: filios quidem: Jacobum, Simo- nem, Judam et Josephum. Filias vero: Esther, Martham et Salomen, que fuit uxor Zebedwi, ma- ter autern Joannis. Hinc.Salvator erat Joannis avunculus, utpote frater Salomes filie Josephi.

---

[10] Bishop of Jerusalem between 634-638
[11] A phraseology meaning the Church of the Holy Sepulcher, being the mother church of Christianity.
[12] This Esther is not mentioned elsewhere in the few texts that relate to the family of Christ. There are various legends regarding women with variants of this name in Christ's family. St. Jerome tells of a certain 'Estha', who was believed to be the first wife of Joseph the Carpenter, and Julius Africanus noted an 'Astha' who married Matthan, grandfather of the aforementioned Joseph.
[13] In Epiphanius of Salamis this name appears as Maria, which is only one letter different in the Greek here. Compare 'Μαρία' to 'Μάρθα'. This might be explained by various scribal errors, but the folk memory appears to be that of the same person.

FRAGMENT IV

The castle of Panormus was founded by Panormus, a certain Greek, built of double walls, and iron mixed together. In its northern gate stood a scaly tower, and a statue of a woman with two arms: where it is to be remembered that something pious happened. For when that castle was burning with fire, and the whole city was razed to the ground together with the walls, that gate of the tower stood in which the statue was placed. Yet, when the fire came closer, as if fleeing, the flame receded five cubits from the statue. This makes for a great story.

A place called Smyrnium nearly quadrupled. It has a hundred porticoes and a subterranean cave of ten cubits towards the north. In it is a new statue, not far from the sacred seat of St. Theodore. Truly, there are in the statues, three [or four], of Constantine the Great, and of his wife Fausta, and of Hilarion the presbyter. The fourth was of Crispin son of Constantine: to whom Herodotus and Hippolytus the chronographer, report that his head was cut off by his father. [Thereafter], his father, moved by the pain of death, spent forty days, as they say, following him in mourning, neither washing his body, nor recuperating himself quietly. He made a statue of pure silver, gilding it with much gold. I think one head of pure gold, inscribed on the front with these words: 'My son, afflicted with injustice'. With this purpose, and with penitence, bowing down religiously, he expounded the pardon of his offenses to God. The rest, however, are seven states: Severus, Barmatius, Xeuxippus, Vigilantii, who built the palaces of Vigilantii, and Eleutherius, who founded a palace for the senate. All these, being drawn to the sword, and erecting statues, implored forgiveness from those who had injured him. And this custom passed to his children, and from them to others, until the time of [the Emperor] Valens the Arian. The Arians, therefore, beholding the defeat which they had received from Constantine, in which we have spoken of in the quadruple portico, to the church of the holy Theodore, the statues were overwhelmed by the earth.

Castrum Panormum a Panormo quodam Greco conditum est, duplici muroconstructum atque ferro &ereque commistum. In ejus porta septentrionali stabat turris squalida, ac biceps muliebris statua : ubi et memorandum quidpiam accidit. Cum enim castrum illud ssvo arderet incendio, ac urbe tota una cum muris solo equata, stetit turris illa porta in qua et statua erat collocata. Sed et sepius igne propius accedente, velut quodam fugante, flamma ab statua ulnas quinque recedebat, Sustulit eam Chosroes Persarum tyrannus, hactenusque in Per- side colitur, uti vivarii prefectus illic captus, ac fuga elapsus declaravit, in Hippoliti Chronico, quod tertio vulgatum est. Quere narrationem eximiam.

Locus nuncupatus Smyrnium, prope quadruplicem porticum, septentrionem versus subterraneam specum habet decem ulnarum : in ea novem statue haud procula sancti Thodori sacra sede. Sunt vero statue, tres [quatuor] quidem Constantini Magni, ejusque uxoris Fausta, et Hilarionis prepositi, 4 quarta Crispi filii Constantini: cui Herodotuset Hippolytus chronographi, tradunt fuisse caput a patre amputatum : cujus et necis dolore affectus pater, dies quadraginta, ut ferunt, eum luctu prosecutus est, nec corpus lavans, necselectuli quiete recreans. Fecit autem statuam ex argento puro, multo auro inaurans: unum caput ex auro puro puto, inscriptis in fronte his verbis: Filius meus in- juria affectus. Hoc ille proposito, sensuque ponitentium more inclinans, religioseque procumbens veniam delictorum a Deo exposcebat. Reliqus au- tem septem (leg. quinque) statum sunt, Severi, Barmati, Xeuxippi, Vigilantii, qui Vigilantii edes exstruxit, et Eleutherii, qui in senatu palatium condidit. Hi omnes gladio animadversi, erectisque statuis, ab eo qui injuria lmserat, veniam exora- bant. Transiitque mos iste in liberos, exque illis in alios, ad usque tempus Valentis Ariani. Ariani itaque, non ferentes quam a Constantino cladem acceperant, in ea quam diximus quadruplici por- ticu, ad sancti. Theodori templum, statuas terra obruerunt.

FRAGMENT V

From Christ's birth to the present of Magi, there are two years. And from the flight into Egypt until the death of Herod the son of Antipater, three years and five days, where they dwelt in Heliopolis in Egypt.

When Joseph and Mary came to Memphis with Jesus, three years and twenty days. After their return to live in Galilee, until the death of Archelaus, there are nine years 47 days. Together with Archelaus, Augustus also dies. He lived for 88 years and ruled for 56 years. From the death of Archelaus, until the baptism of Christ, which he received from John in the Jordan, are 16 years and 30 days. From the baptism, until the stoning of Zachariah, one year. He was doing sacred work as was customary. When they stoned him they twisted his head and killed him. And having taken his body, they hanged him in the valley of Josaphat. For John the Baptist lived sixty-six years. He spent thirty years in the desert, but for others, he administered baptism in the Jordan, preaching penance. Thus, the Lord Jesus Christ lived in the thirtieth year of his age.

After his baptism, he was withdrawn. He received and chose His disciples, and with them, He proclaimed His kingdom until His salutary passion for three years. After this, the canons of the Synod of Nicaea, three hundred and eighteen divine Fathers, made their decision that after the age of thirty, none of the priests should be accused of the order. For it is sufficient, they say, for the disciple to be like his teacher and for the servant to be like his master.

From the saving passion and the ascension of Christ, until the stoning of St. Stephen, the first martyr, until the light which Saul saw and appeared to him, were six months. And from the light which appeared to Saul, and from his baptism and preaching, until the 88th birthday of the holy Virgin Mary, three years and thirty-three days.

She lived in the most holy lands of Deipara the virgin for a total of 59 years. She received instructions from the Archangel Gabriel, and when she conceived our Lord Jesus Christ, she gave birth to Him on the 25th of December, aged 15 years. In the house of John the Evangelist, she lived for 11 years. Indeed, the time was all the years of the life of the virgin and mother [of God], sixty-one. It is this John, whom the Lord loved, who was a virgin, who also wrote the Gospel, and remained in Jerusalem in the holy mountain of Zion. Known as the mother of all temples, this was his abode. Thereafter, the apostles, for fear of the Jews, took refuge. There, with the doors closed, the Lord appeared to His disciples after he had risen from the dead, and He gave them the Holy Spirit and peace. There, on the eighth day, when Thomas was nodding, the Lord gave him a certain wound in his side, and the shape of the nails and the image shown. There, the paschal lamb was prepared for our Lord, the Shepherd, which He would eat with His disciples. They also went out from there to the place called 'Gethsemane'. In that first holy Eucharist, Christ completed its mystery, delivered it to His disciples, taught the mystic worship, and received the tonsure given to the clergy. He then spent the benefit of the blessing, initiated with the sacred orders the whole of all the mysteries which He gave in the commandments and set forth the series of His majesty, the glory which He divinely gave in His form. To the blessed, to whom He gazed upon, He exhibited a spectacle, as He was the Church's magnificence, adornment, and splendor, as well as. He deigned to share them in the divine communion of his body and blood; as Nicodemus [...][14] Zachariah, who had been the father of John the Baptist, the son of Berachiah the son of Abijah, the priest of the forerunner of Christ. And at that time indeed Joseph was a widower, so that Salome and John the Baptist were children of true brothers. Indeed, Haggai, son of Berachiah, was John's uncle. Zachariah, the brother of Haggai, was Salome's uncle; whom Joseph the carpenter had in marriage. I mean Salome, not that midwife, but Joseph's wife. For the midwife was a native of Bethlehem, and Elizabeth herself a cousin, and the most sacred of the Virgin Mary. The Gospel declares this

---

[14] The source text here is illegible

in the holy light. For there were three sisters in Bethlehem, the daughter of the priest Mathan, and his wife Mari, who lived during the reign of Queen Cleopatra and Sopalor of Persia, and that before Herod the son of Antipater obtained the Jewish kingdom. The first name was Mary, the second name was Soms[15], the third was called Anna. She married first in Bethlehem, and gave birth to Salome, a midwife. The other was married there, and [Soms] she gave birth to Elizabeth. She married the third in Galilee, and gave birth to Mary Deipara: so that Salome, Elisabeth, and Saint Mary Deipara are the daughters of three sisters. Since he is the brother of his own children, not only from the fact that he was nurtured and educated together, but also from Haggai, the brother of Zachariah, kinship of the priest.

Our Lord Jesus Christ is therefore born from the tribe of Judah and from the seed of David, according to human His nature. Born in the last days, 6000 years from the creation of the world, in the forty-second year of Augustus the emperor, in the month December, on the 25th at four in the evening.

It must also be known that from the beginning, according to the Hebrew understanding, the origin of the world, at the beginning and the end, from the first man Adam until Noah (under whom the flood existed, and there are ten generations) 2142 years. So are the many generations, the years are 1270. Abraham was 75 years old when he migrated from Mesopotamia to the land of Canaan: and he stayed there for 25 years, and begat his son Isaac. Isaac was born in the sixtieth year of 5880, he has two children, Esau and Jacob, who was in Egypt with his twelve sons and grandsons. They numbered seven hundred and thirty-five. And his people dwelt in the land of Canaan for two hundred and fifteen years, and later in Egypt. When they had inhabited it for as many years, and having taken the increase, it was reported in twelve tribes, and the heads being counted, they filled a thousand kilos. Levi was indeed had descendants, Moses and Aaron. And this was indeed a priest [...]

---

[15] This appear to be a textual corruption of the name given elsewhere as "Sobe"

Ten periods or revolutions, beginning at the beginning of the first century, and ending in the sixteenth year of the sixteenth century itself. Therefore, enumerating these periods, the tenth was completed in the year 5320. And from the beginnings of the eleventh period, one hundred and eighty six years passed, and our Lord Jesus Christ was put on a human nature, as the book of Nicomedia and the Metaphrastes have. Yet, Basil the Great says that in the five thousandth and fiftieth year our Lord Jesus Christ was born. Thus, from the above-mentioned eleventh period, the sixth millennium.

The rest of the writers, such as Eusebius, Eustathius, George Chronologus, and others put and epoch around four-hundred and eighty years. He spent thirty-three years spent in the world and the life of the world, and the community, and for the sake of our salvation suffered death. On the 23rd of March he was nailed to the cross. He was buried on the second and on the 25th he rose again, on the first day, on Sunday, as Metaphrastes declares, from Nicoinediensis, stating that it was on April 2nd, which was the day he rose from the dead.

In fact, I have the same feeling for Lord Simeohis, since the labor of this world began from the 22nd of March: the light (of the sun) by which we measure everything, was created by God on the fourth day of the same month, 23rd. For hence what are ten and seventies ten, and also fifty: the number of the attendants in the court. It must be carefully considered; he was half God by his divine wisdom. In seven centuries, he founded the world, and it was made in seven days. He gave Cain gave the mark seven times, and of Lamech the seventy-seven times. The seventy-seventh is numbered from Adam. Even Pentecost, or the fiftieth jubilee (of the year) (you will say remission) is therefore in honor. In the seventh month also, they prepared those solemn sacrifices.

Yet, if you want to find the dimensions around the course of the sun and the moon: take the period, draw it through seven times ten and four times ten, through the dimension of the sun and the moon, and you will prove that safely, and the zither will fall. In turn, and roll the orb, and inside, they are written and marked, and you will find the disk stored for years, until the coming of Christ. And henceforth again the genealogy of Christ's becoming man for us, and the periods of the sun and moon. and the paschal beginnings, and the immediate ends, as they are written about under Constantine.

Christinativitate usque ad Magoruin prasen- tiam, anni sunt duo. Et a fuga in Egyptum, usque ad mortem Herodis filii Antipatri, anni tres, dies quinque. Habitarunt autem in Egypto Heliopoli, qua ad Memphin.

Joseph et Maria cum Jesu, annis tribus, diebus 20. Post ipsorum vero regressum, ut in Galilasa habitarent, usque ad mortem Archelai, anni sunt 9, dies 47. Una cum Archelao Augustus quoque moritur. Vixit vero annis 88, et imperavit annis 56. Ab Archelai porro morte, usque ad Christi baptismum, quem a Joanne in Jordane accepit, anni sunt 16, dies 30. A baptismo, usque ad Zacharis lapidationem, annus unus. (Interea enim, dum sacris ipse operaretur de more, lapidibus jactis, etin caput contortis, eum trucidarunt: corporeque raptato in valle Josaphat suspenderunt.) À Zacharis autem lapidatione, usque ad Joannis filii ipsius mortem, sub Herode Juniore, Archelai filio in carcerepatratam, annus unus. A morte Joannis, usque ad salvificam passionem, menses 6. Trigginta enim et sex annos Joannes Baptista vixit. Triginta quidem annuis versatus est in deserto: aliis vero 6 in Jordane baptismum administrabat, predicans penitentiam. Sic Dominus jesus Christus, tricesimum etatis sue annum agebat. Post baptismum yero receplum, ascivit sibi delegitque discipulos, cum iisdem suum regnum promulgans usque ad salutiferam passionem, annis tribus. Idcirco Nicanm synodi trecentorum duodeviginti divorum Patrum canones jubent, decernuntque; utante annum 30, nullusin presbyterorum allegeretur ordinem. Sufficit enim, aiunt, discipulo,ut sit sicut magister ipsius: et servo,ut sit sicut ejus dominus.

A salvifica vero passione, et ascensione Christi, usque ad sancti Stephani primi martyris lapidationem, usque ad lucem, qua Saulo visa et, eique apparuit, menses sunt sex: alque a luce, qua ipsi Saulo apparuit, et ab ejusdem baptismo et praedicatione, usque ad sancte Marie Virginis 88 sumplionem, anni tres, dies 33. Vixit autem in terria sanctissima Deipara oĭ Virgo, annis 59. Et hoc quidem pacto: In templo annis 14, in domo Jaseph mensibus 8, statimque salutata est, et divini partus internuntium a Gabriele archangelo accepit: et cum concepisset Dominum nostrum Jesum Christum, peperit eumdem 20 Decembris die... annos nata 15. Vixit vero Domino nostro Jesu Christo,in humana natura hic vivente annis 33. Post Domini autem assumptionem et ascensionem, cum ipsius discipulis,in domo Joannis evangeliste, vixit annis 11, dies sunt vero anni omnes vite ipsius virginis et matris, undesexaginta. Hic porro ipse est Joannes, quem diligebat Dominus, qui virgo fuit: qui et Evangelium conscripsit, quique perstitit Hierosolymis in sancta 6 Sionis dicta, templorum omnium matre, hoc ipsius erat domicilium. llluc igitur apostoli, propter metum Judaeorum, confugerunt. Illic foribus clausis,discipulis suis apparuit Dominus, posteaquam a mortuis exstitit: et Spiritum sanctum, et pacem eisdem dedit. Illic die octavo Thomam nutantem certum reddidit Dominus lateris sui plaga, et clavorum forma, et effigie demonstrata. Illic Domino Bervatori nostro paschalis agnus, quem cum suis ederet discipulis, fuit apparatus. Etiam inde in locum Gethsemane dictum, egressi sunt. lbidem primo sanctam Eucharistie mysterium confecit Christus, suisque discipulis tradidit, mysticum cultum edocuit, et tonsura data in clerum ascivit, benedictionis beneficium impendit,sacris Ordinibus initiavit totam omnium arcanorum, que in mandatis dabat, et majestatis sui seriem exposuit, gloriam que divine sua forme, beatorumque, à quibus spectatur, spectaculum exhibuit. ut et magniticentiam, ornatum, splendoremque Ecclesiv sum: eosdem divina corporis et sanguinis sui communione dignatus est; ut et Nicodeman [...] Zacharis, qui fuerat pater Joannis Baptiste, Christi Prodromi, filii Barachise, filii Abia sacerdotis. Et tunc quidem viduus erat Joseph, ut Salome, et Joannes Baptista fratrum germanorum sint liberi. Etenim Aggeus,Barachie, filius, patruus erat Joannis. Zachariasitem, frater Aggai, patruus erat Salomes; quam Joseph faber in matrimonio habebat. Salomen autem dico, non obstetricem illam, sed Josephi conjugem. Obstetrix enim e Bethleem erat oriunda, et ipsa consobrina Elisabeth, et sacrosancte Virginis Marie. Idque sancti Luce declarat Evangelium. Tres enim sorores erant Bethleemitice, sacerdotis Mathan filie, et uxoris illius Mari& ; regnante Cleopatra regina, et Sopalore

Persa, idque antequam Herodes filius Antipatri regnum Judaicum obtineret. Nomen prime erat Maria ; nomen secunde Soms: tertia dicebatur Anna. Prima nupsit in Bethleem, et Salomen obstetricem genuit. Altera ibidem nuptui fuit tradita, et Elisa. betham peperit. Tertia in Galilea nupsit,et Mariam Deiparam genuit : ut Salome,et Elisabeth,et sancta Maria Deipara trium sororum sint filise.Atque hinc Joannes Baptista, ct Christus Dominus noster, consobrini esse dicuntur: filius vero Joseph esse ferebatur. Quoniam filiorum ipsius frater est, non ex eo solum, quod una fuerit nutritus, eteducatus, verum etiam ex Aggmi fratris Zacharis; sacerdotis cognatione Nascitur itaque Dominus noster Jesus Christus ex tribu Juda et e semine David, secundum humanam naturam, diebus postremis, 6000 a creatione mundi anno, 42 Augusti imperatoris anno, mense Decembri 25, noctis hora 16 die 1.

Sciendum vero etiam illud, ut a primordio, secundum Hebream computationem,mundi demonstres originem, tolle, atque aufer, a protoplasto Adam, ad usque Noe (sub quo diluvium exstitit, suntque generationes decem) annos 2142. Simili pacto a diluvio usque ad Abraham, generationes totidem, anni sunt 1270. Abraham porro annorum erat 75, quando ex Mesopotamia in Chananeam terram commigravit: ibique annis 25 demoratus, Isaac filium progenuit. Sexagesimum annum 5880 natus, duos liberos Esau et Jacob obtinet.

Egyptum cum duodecim suis filiis, et nepotibus.

numero 735 subiit. Habitavit autem ipsius gens in terra Chanaan, annis 215. Deinde Egyptum. cum annis totidem incoluisset, et incremento capto, in duodecim tribus esset relata, capita autem computata, mille chiliades expleverunt. Levi quidem posteri, Moses et Aaron fuere.Et hic quidem sacerdo [...] decim periodis sive revolutionibus, orsis a primi seculi primordio, et in ipso sex millesimo, decimo sexto anno desinentibus. Enumerando igitur hàs periodos, decima completa est anno 5320. De incepta autem undecima periodo, 186 anni abierunt, et humanam naturam induit Dominus noster Jesus Christus, ut liber Nicomediensis et Metaphrastes habent. Magnus vero Basilius dicit, ipso quinquies millesimo, quingentesimo anno Dominus noster

Jesus Christus nascitur.Itaque ex supra dicta undecima periodo supersuntahhni sex.Reliqui scriptores, ut Eusebius Pamphili, Eustathius, Georgius Chronologi, et alli 480 duntaxat annos putaht et slatüunt. Alii, ahhos... triginta tres annos in mundo et liac vita versatus, et comtnoratüs, et propter salutem nostram mortem passus, 23 Martii fuit cruci affixus. Die 2& sepultus; et 25 resufrexit, die priinà, tiimirürn Doriüinica, velut Metaphrastes declarat, el Nicoinediensis : sed ul ceeteri, Aprilis 2| die a mortuis exstitit. Equidem fldem habeo senteriti: domini Siméohis : quippe mundi hujus molitio ab 22 Marlii mensis Initiutmi accepit: lux ilem (solis) qua metimur omnia, ejusdem mensis 23 quarto die füit condita divinitus. Hinc enim qualer decem et septias decem, tum quinquagesi: mus numerus suht in hofiore. Et attente considerandum est; duoniam Deus divina sua sapientia; in 7 szculis mundum fundavit: septemque diebus est fabricatus, et de Cain dedit ültlonem septies, de Lamech autem septuagies septies.Etioch seplimum transtülit, velut eum, qui Deo placeret : Abrahiam etiam a mundi constitutione, multaruin gentium patrem declaravit : sed et ipse Dominus septuagesimus septimus ab Adam numeratur. Etiam Pentecoste, seu Quinquagesima jubilei (anni) (remissionem dixeris) idcirco est in honore. Septimo quoque mense solemhia illa sacrificia paragebantnr.

Quod si voles et circa solis, luneque cursum, reperire dimensionem : cape periodum, el subduc per septies decem perque quater decem, per solis et lune dimensionem idque tuto,citraque lapsum probabis. [n gyrum autem, et orbem volve,quee intus,
scripta, et notata sunt, et invenies orbis conditi
annos,ad Christi usque adventum. Et posthac rursum Christi pro nobis hominis facti genealogiam, et solis,ac lunz periodos. paschalesque incipientes, et instantes terminos, prout sub Constantino de scripti sunt.

FRAGMENT VI

Zacharias, the father of John, had a brother, a priest named Haggai, who died before him. The daughter of this Haggai married Joseph the Carpenter; by whom he had four sons and three daughters; one of whom was James, who is known as the brother of the Lord; and was the first bishop of Jerusalem. The name of Joseph's wife was Salome, not the midwife, but another. After her death, Joseph asked for his wife, Maria Deipara, who descended from Matthan the priest, just as Joseph descended from Solomon, the son of David. This all happened as the Gospel of Luce mentioned it as weaving a genealogy. The blessed Matthan had daughters by Mary, his wife, whose names were Mary, Sube, and Anna. Mary [the eldest] therefore gave birth to Elizabeth, the mother of John the Baptist. Anna gave birth to the blessed Deipara in Bethlehem, after which Mary was called from the name of her grandmother and mother. Truly, Elizabeth is indeed Anne's cousin, and the daughter of Deipara's kin. Both of these are confirmed from the Gospel, because it enumerates the paternal and carnal race of Christ. For [Luke] says, Jesus was about 30 years old, and was supposed to be [the son of] Joseph, [the son of] Heli-Mathan.

Zacharias pater Joannis fratrem habuit consacerdotem nomine Aggaum, qui ante illum mortuus est. Hujus Aggai filiam duxit uxorem Joseph faber, ex qua genuit IV filios et III filias: quorum unus erat Jacobus, qui cognominatur frater Domini, fuitque primus Hierosolymorum episcopus. Nomen uxoris Joseph Salome, non quidem obstetrix illa, sed alia. Post mortem autem ejus, uxorem sibi postulat Josephus Mariam Deiparam, qua ex materno genere descendebat a Matthan sacerdote, et ipso a Salomone Davidis filio, ut dicit Evangelium Luce genealogiam texens. ste Matthan filias habuit ex Maria conjuge sua, quarum nomina Maria, Sube, Anna Maria itaque parit Elsabetham matrem Joannis Baptisue: Anna parit sanctam Deiparam in Bethlehem, qua Maria vocata est de nomine avie et materter; adeo ut sit Elisabet consobrina quidem Anne, filia vero fratris Deipa. Ex Evangelio hec utraque con firmantur, propterea quod recenseat genus paternum et carnale

Christi: Erat enim, inquit, Jesus incipiens, quasi annorum 30, qui putabatur
Josephi, Heli Mathan.

FRAGMENT VII

Hippolytus of Thebans from his chronological syntagma.

It must be known that from Adam to barbarism, there are 2266 years, and from barbarism to Scythism, five hundred years, and from Scythism to Hellenism, 1236 years, and from Hellenism to Judaism, a thousand years, and from Judaism to Christianity, five hundred years. Starting with the whole calculation, we find that from Adam to Christ is 5050 years and from the birth of our Lord Jesus Christ to Constantine the Great, 200 years.

Moreover, it should be known that from Adam, the first parent of mankind, to Noah, under whom the flood occurred, there are ten generations, or 2451 years. Adam is interpreted by the four letters of the alphabet, East, West, North, and South.

From the flood to Abraham, when he migrated to the land of Canaan from Mesopotamia, there are ten generations, or 1121 years. Abraham was then 73 years old, and settled in the land of Canaan for 25 years and begot Isaac. But Isaac, when he was sixty years old, begat two sons, Esau and Jacob.

Jacob, when he was one hundred and thirty years old, went down into Egypt together with his twelve sons and grandsons. Levi's descendants were Moses and Aaron. This priesthood is from him, for he is prefect of the government of the nation. The law took effect three days after his departure from Egypt, and they stayed in the desert for forty years.

The reign of Joshua, [son of] Nun, was for twenty-five years, from the Judges for 450 years until the reign of Saul. Next came David, the father [of the nation], and there were fourteen generations from Abraham to David, or 1924 years. And from David to the transmigration of Babylon, fourteen generations, or 304 years. We find that it is a total of 10,210 years from Adam to Christ.

Christ is born in the forty-second year of Augustus the Emperor, on the 10th month of the 7th day[16]. [He was born] from the tribe of Judah, from the seed of David according to the flesh. After so many years, how is he not ashamed of Plato disputing about the first and the second flood?

Scire oportet, quod ab Adam usque ad barbarismum, sunt anni 2266 et a barbarismo usque ad scythesmum, anni 500 eta scythesmo usque ad Hellenismum, anni 1236 et ab Hellenismo usque ad Judaismum, anni mille: et ab Judaismo usque ad Christianismum, anni quingenti. Inito universim calculo, invenimus ab Adam ad Christum annos 100190 et a nativitate Domini nostri Jesu Christi ad Constantinum magnum annos 200. Preterea sciendum, quod a primo hominum parente Adam usque ad Noe, sub quo contigit diluvium, sunt generationes decem, seu anni 2451. Adam per quatuor alphabeti litteras interpretatur Oriens, Occidens, Septentrio et Meridies.

A diluvio usque ad Abraham, quando transmigravit in terram Chanaan de Mesopotamia, sunt generationes 10 vel anni 1121. Erat tunc Abraham,

---

[16] January 6th or 7th

annorum 73, incoluitque Chanandcam terram annos 25, et genuit Isaac. Isaac vero natus annos Lx genuit duos filios, Esau et Jacob.

Jacob, cum esset annorum 130, descendit in egyptum una cum duodecim filiis suis et nepotibus 4, 7 smero 75 mansitque Jacob in Egypto aunos 400, multiplicata,reputata est iu duodecim tribus,et multitudo populi in sexcenta millia.

Levi posteri fuere Moyses et Aaron. Hic sacerdotio decoratusest, ille regimini gentis preeficitur. Ita- que anno vito suc octogesimo calcat mare Rubrum. Legum latio cepit triduo post egressum de Agypto. Mansere in deserto annos 40.

Reguntura Jesu Nave annos 25, ab Judicibus annos 450 usque ad regnum Saul. Deinceps venit David socer illius. Fueruntque ab Abraham ad David generationes 14 vel anni 1924. Et a David ad transmigrationem Babylonis, generationes 14 vel anni 304, universim inito calculo reperimus ab Adam ad Christum annos 10210.
Christus nascitur quadragesimo secundo anno Augusti imperatoris,indiclione 10, feria 7, ex tribu Juda ex semine David secundum carnem. Cum porro tot sint anni, quomodo non pudet Platonem disserentem de diluvio primo et secundo

FRAGMENT VIII

A chronicle of the incarnation of our Lord Jesus Christ, the great God and our Savior.

Our Lord was born of Deipara, the ever-virgin Mary, in the year three hundred and ninety-fourth Olympiad. This was the 42nd year of the Emperor Augustus, and the 32nd year of the reign of Herod [son of] Antipater. Augustus reigned 56 years, and Herod 37 years.

Therefore, Herod died when our Lord had been in the flesh six years, but Archelaus, his son, reigned after Herod, and was sent into exile in Gaul. Antipas, the son of Herod [son of] Antipater, reigned. When Augustus died, and Archelaus was sent into exile, Christ was 15 years old from his incarnation[17]. Tiberius succeeded Augustus, and Antipas, the son of Herod, also succeeded Archelaus. They are therefore found to have reigned at the same time, Tiberius of Quidene, over the Romans, and Antipas, the son of Herod over the Jews, as has been said. The first year of the reign of Tiberius and Herod is found to have been the sixteenth year of Christ from his incarnation. Therefore, in the fifteenth year of the reign of Tiberius, the Lord was thirty years old from His incarnation when He came to the baptism of John and received the divine preaching, as the most divine Luke says. In the 19th year of the reign of Tiberius, the divine crucifixion and the living resurrection took place. And Antipas, the son of Herod, reigned for twenty-three years. Hence, it is certain that this Herod killed the forerunner, and at the time of the divine passion existing in Jerusalem judged the Lord. After a lively restoration he reigned another five years, and was sent into exile with Herodias to Vienna. [Herod] Agrippa, who was also the son of Herod, son of Aristobulus by Mariamne, the first wife of Herod[18], succeeded him. Now

---

[17] This would place the birth of Christ around the year 9 BC.
[18] Not his first wife, but his chief wife, as his first marriage was to Doris the Idumean.

Agrippa, who was also Herod, killed James [son] of Zebedee. Yet, Peter, the coryphseur[19] of the Apostles, wanted to kill him, so that he might be gratified to Jude. Moreover, he also reigned seven years, and after him, another Agrippa reigned, under whom Paul was judged in Caesarea by Festus in the year 30 [after the death of Christ].

After this, Titus conquered Jerusalem and as 40 years had passed, from the passion of the Savior until the capture of Jerusalem. Some have written that three hundred martyrs died there. Indeed, the siege lasted for two years, so that they ate their children to avoid starvation.

Chronicon de incarnatione Domini nostri Jesu Christi magni Dei, et Salvatoris nostri.

Natus est Dominus noster ex Deipara et seniper Virgine Maria, anno tertio centesimw nonazesime quarl: Olympiadis. Is vero erat 42 annus Augusti imperatoris, regni vero Herodis Antipatri 32. Regnavit autem Augustus annis 56, Herodes vero 37.

Igitur mortuus est Herodes quando Dominus noster sex annos habebatin carne. Regnavit vero post Herodem Archelaus fllius ejus an 9,et missus est in exsilium in Galliam,et regnavit Antipas filius et ipse Herodis Antipatri. Mortuo vero Augusto, et Archelao in exsilium misso, habebat Christus ab incarnatione annos 15. Augusto vero successit Tiberius, Antipas autem fllius quoque Herodis successit Archelao. Reperiuntur igitur simul regnasse, super Romanos quideni Tiberius, super Judemos vero Herodis fllius Antipas, uti dictum est. Primus annus regni Tiberii, et Herodis reperitur fuisse decimus sextus annus Christi ab incarnatione ejus. His vero ita se habentibus, anno regni Tiberii decimo quinto, Dominus habebat ab incarnatione annos 30, quando venit ad baptisma Joannis, et cepit divinam praedicationem, ut ait divinissimus Lucas. Regni vero Tiberii anno 19, divina érucifixio, et viviflca

---

[19] A leader of a chorus of men

resurtectio facta est. Antipas vero ille Hetodis filius regnavit annis 23. Certum proinde est, quod hic Herodes Precursorem occiderit, et tempore divine passionis in Jerusalem exsistens judicarit Dominum; et post viviflcam resütrectiotiem regnarit aliis quinque annis, et in exsilium missus sit cum Herodiade in Viennam. Hegnavit vero post ipsum Agrippa qui et Herodis, filius Aristobuli ex Mariamne primi Herodis fllii. Hic autem Agrippa, qui et Herodes, occidit Jacobum Zebedmi. Petrum vero Apostolorum coryphseurh voluit occidere, ut gratiflcaretur Judemis. Porro et ille regnavit septem annis, et post ipsum regnavit alter Agrippa, sub quo Paulus in Cesarea judicatus est a Festo anno 30.

Et post hec Titus expugnavit Hierosolymam: simul autem sumpti sunt anni 40, a passione Salvatoris usque ad capturam Hierosolymorum. Quidam veto scribunt, in ea occubuisse ad trecentas myriadas: duravit vero obsidio illius, annis duobus, ita ut infantes suos pre fame manducaverint.

FRAGMENT IX

It helps to know that the holy Gospel of Matthew was written in Palestine, in Hebrew, in the eighth year after the assumption of Christ[20]. The Gospel of Mark was written by a man in the twelfth year after the Assumption[21]. The Gospel of Luke was written in Greece, in the great [city of] Alexandria in the fifteenth year after the Assumption[22]. The Gospel of John was written in Greece on the island of Patmos[23], in the thirty-second year after the Assumption[24].

Scire juvat, quod sanctum Matthaei Evangelium scriptum est in Palestina hebraice, octavo post Christi assumptionem anno. Marci Evangelium laune scriptum est Homme anno post assumptionem duodecimo. Luc Evangelium scriptum est Grece in magna Alexandria anno decimo quinto post assumptionem. Evangelium Joannis scriptum Greece est in Patmo insula, áànno post assumptionem tricesimo secundo.

---

[20] That is in the year 41 AD.
[21] That is in the year 45 AD.
[22] That is in the year 48 AD.
[23] He is confusing John the Evangelist with John of Patmos.
[24] That is in the year 65 AD.

FRAGMENT X

Hippolytus concerning the twelve apostles, where each of them preached, and where he was finished.

Hippolyti de duodecim apostolis, ubinam quisque eorum pradicaverit, ac ubi consummatus sit.

FRAGMENT XI

The same Hippolytus concerning the seventy apostles.

Ejusdem Hippolyti de septuaginta apostolis.

FRAGMENT XII

The fathers of the twelve apostles and their names by whom they were born.

Duodecim apostolorum patrig et eorum nomina quibus sunt nati.

FRAGMENT XIII

Our Lord Jesus was born according to the flesh of Christ from our glorious Lady, holy of God, Mother and ever Virgin Mary, in the year 1010, and of the year forty-three of Augustus Caesar in Bethlehem Judea, which was the 6th of January of the Romans, or that of December 25. He was baptized when He was thirty years old, in the fifteenth year of Tiberius Caesar, the day before mid-January according to the Romans, which is January 6th. It is necessary to know that the city of Bethlehem gave birth to Him according to the flesh. The city of Nazareth nourished Him, brought Him to manhood, and the city of Capernaum retained His at the age of thirty. His form was as follows: His stature was that of a just man, neither surpassing those of measure, nor falling short of the contrary. He did not in the least overflow with flesh. His hair was long and all curled, which is to say that His hair was turned up. He was circumcised, that is to say, having an infinite caesarean, or with promised hair, parted locks in front of the forehead, with a nose, sallow, black pupils of the eyes, long fingers, a moderate mustache or beard of the lips, exhibiting this not by the lowering of the hair but by a dignified conversion. After thirty years, when He had chosen His disciples, and for three years had preached the divine and Holy Gospel. Then finally, He was crucified for us voluntarily under Pontius Pilate in the 19th year of Tiberius Caesar, on the tenth day of April according to the Roman calendar, which is the 23rd day of March. And when He rose in the morning, in April, which is March 25th, on the 4th day, He was taken up again from where He had descended on the third day, being May the 5th.

Natus est secundum carnem Dominus noster Jesus Christus ex gloriosa Domina nostra sancta Dei. Genitrice semperque Virgine Maria,anno 1010, Augusti Cesaris anno 43 in Bethlehem Jude 8 Kal. Januarias juxta Romanos, hoc est Decembris 25. Baptizatus est 30 annos agens, anno quintodecimo Tiberii Caesaris, pridie Id. Januar. secundum Romanos, lioc est Januar. 6. Oportet autem scire, quod genuit illum secundum carnem civitas Bethlehem,enutrivit urbs Nazareth, ad virilem tatem perduxit retinuitque ad annos 30 civitas Capernaum. Elfigies forme illius erat hujusmodi: Magnitudo stature illius justi hominis erat, neque mensurani superans, neque in contrarium deficiens, minime redundabat carnibus; magna erat coma totaque cincinnata, id est,revolutis capillis; intonsus, infinitam nempe cesariem habens, sive promissis capillis, bifariam ante frontem discriminatus cincinnos, nasutus, subflavus, nigris oculorum pupillis, longis digitis, mediocri mystacio seu labiorum barba,non demissione pilorum hanc promittens, sed decora conversione venerabilis. Post 30 annos vero cum discipulos elegisset, ac per triennium predicasset divinum sanctumque Evangelium, tunc demum cruci suffixus est sponte pro nobis sub Pontio Pilato, anno 19 Tiberii Cwsaris, decimo Kal. April. Juxta Romanos, id est Martii die 23 feria 6. Et cum resurrexisset mane, Kal. Aprilis, id est Martii 25,feria 4,etiam assumptus iterum est eo unde descenderat, die tertia Mai, feria v.

D.P. Curtin is a psychologist, philologist, and translator of ancient texts. He obtained his A.B. from Villanova University in 20007, his M.S. from Chestnut Hill College in 2014, and his Psy.D from Chatham University in 2023. He also has academic coursework through Philadelphia College of Osteopathic Medicine and the Philadelphia School of Psychoanalysis. He resides in Brandywine, DE with his wife and family.

Other works of translation by D.P. Curtin:

First Book of Ethiopian Maccabees (2018)

On Fate by Albertus Magnus (2022)

Book of Josippon (2023)

About Fifteen Problems by Albertus Magnus (2023)

www.ingramcontent.com/pod-product-compliance
Lightning Source LLC
Chambersburg PA
CBHW070956120626
46546CB00004B/1642